SPORTS
ALL-STARS

LUKE KUECHLY

Matt Doeden

Lerner Publications ◆ Minneapolis

Lerner Publications Company
A division of Lerner Publishing Group, Inc.
241 First Avenue North
Minneapolis, MN 55401 USA

For reading levels and more information, look up this title at www.lernerbooks.com.

Main body text set in Albany Std 15/22. Typeface provided by Agfa.

Library of Congress Cataloging-in-Publication Data

Names: Doeden, Matt, author.
Title: Luke Kuechly / Matt Doeden.
Description: Minneapolis : Lerner Publications, [2017] | Series: Sports All-Stars |
    Includes bibliographical references and index.
Identifiers: LCCN 2016020552 (print) | LCCN 2016028607 (ebook) | ISBN
    9781512425840 (lb : alk. paper) | ISBN 9781512431216 (pb : alk. paper) | ISBN
    9781512428292 (eb pdf)
Subjects: LCSH: Kuechly, Luke, 1991–—Juvenile literature. | Football players—
    United States—Biography—Juvenile literature. | Carolina Panthers (Football
    team)—History—Juvenile literature.
Classification: LCC GV939.K84 D64 2017 (print) | LCC GV939.K84 (ebook) | DDC
    796.332092 [B] —dc23

LC record available at https://lccn.loc.gov/2016020552

Manufactured in the United States of America
1-41352-23296-9/2/2016

CONTENTS

Luke Kuechly
led the Carolina
Panthers in
tackles in 2015.

Carolina Panthers middle linebacker Luke Kuechly peered at Russell Wilson of the Seattle Seahawks. Seattle's quarterback barked signals to his teammates. It was the first quarter of a National Football League (NFL) playoff game on January 17, 2016. Moments earlier, the Panthers had taken a 7–0 lead.

Wilson took the ball and stepped back to pass. He saw Seattle running back Marshawn Lynch run into the open. Wilson fired. But Kuechly knew the pass was coming before Wilson even threw it.

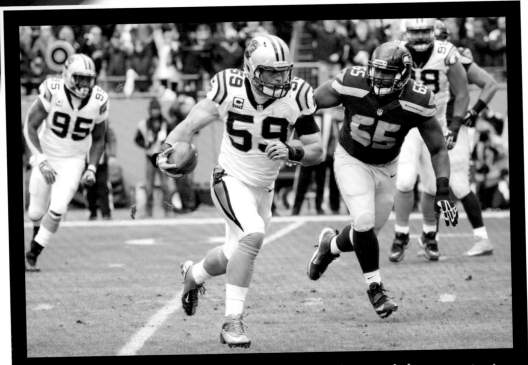

Kuechly runs the ball to the end zone. The touchdown against Seattle was the second touchdown of his NFL career.

Kuechly was ready. He stepped forward. He intercepted the pass and took off running. He sprinted to the right and outran the Seahawks. Touchdown! The crowd roared as Kuechly celebrated with his teammates.

The great play was just the start for Kuechly and the Panthers. His 11 tackles were the most on the team as the Panthers beat the Seahawks, 31–24. In the next playoff game, Kuechly did it again. He intercepted a pass from Arizona Cardinals quarterback Carson Palmer and scored another touchdown. Carolina crushed Arizona, 49–15.

This was just the latest highlight for the young linebacker. In his brief four-year career, Kuechly had already been voted to three **Pro Bowls**. After helping beat the Cardinals, his next big game would be the Super Bowl.

Kuechly (left) and his teammates celebrate after beating the Cardinals to reach the 2016 Super Bowl.

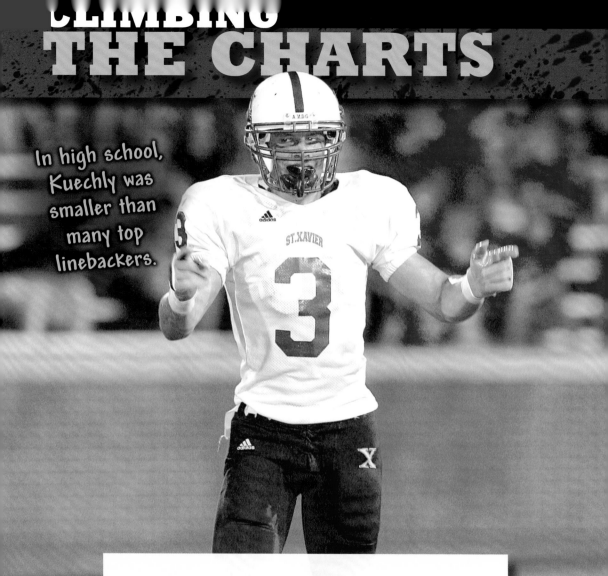

In high school, Kuechly was smaller than many top linebackers.

In 2008, Luke Kuechly began his senior year at St. Xavier High School in Cincinnati, Ohio. He wasn't a top football **recruit** at the time.

Scouts label the top high school football players in the United States as five-star recruits. Four-star recruits are next and are still highly prized by colleges. Three-star recruits are thought of as players who might have a shot to play major college football. But they aren't expected to be stars.

Then there was Kuechly. He was a two-star recruit. Major colleges in the area such as Ohio State and Notre Dame weren't interested in him. Few scouts gave him much chance to excel in the college game, much less the NFL.

Many scouts thought Kuechly was too small to be a linebacker and too

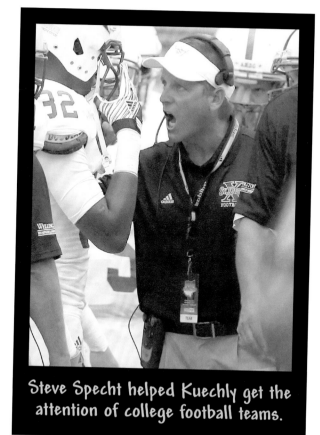

Steve Specht helped Kuechly get the attention of college football teams.

slow to be a **safety**. But his high school coach, Steve Specht, knew Kuechly could succeed in college. "All I kept saying to [college scouts] was . . . '[Kuechly] is one of the best football players I've ever had,'" Specht said. A great senior season bumped Kuechly's rating up to three stars. That got the attention of a few major college programs. Kuechly chose Boston College (BC) in Chestnut Hill, Massachusetts.

In 2009, Kuechly wasn't expected to play much for BC as a freshman. But that changed before the season. BC's starting linebacker, Mark Herzlich, left the team with an illness. Then sophomore Will Thompson suffered

Mark Herzlich was one of college football's top linebackers. In 2009, he learned he had a rare form of cancer. Herzlich recovered and returned to BC in 2010. He went on to become a starting linebacker for the NFL's New York Giants.

an injury. Suddenly, 18-year-old Kuechly was the team's starting **outside linebacker**.

Kuechly was small for the college game. But he was quick and had a natural instinct for football. It didn't take him long to prove that he was much better than most three-star recruits. Kuechly became a tackling machine for BC. He went on to lead the team and the **Atlantic Coast Conference (ACC)** with 87 tackles in 2009. "It really is amazing," said senior linebacker Mike

Kuechly receives a trophy as the Most Valuable Player (MVP) on defense for BC in the 2009 Emerald Bowl.

Kuechly spreads his arms for a tackle. He proved at BC that he was good enough to play in the NFL.

McLaughlin. "Playing the linebacker position at that young an age . . . it's very difficult to do."

The good season was only the beginning for Kuechly. In 2010, he moved to middle linebacker. It's a position that some call the quarterback of the defense. He thrived in his new role. Kuechly's 183 tackles that year were the most by any player in college football.

Then, in 2011, he set a new career high with 191 tackles. For the second year in a row, Kuechly had the most tackles in college football. It was also the most in

Boston College history. He won the Butkus Award as the nation's top linebacker.

After three seasons at BC, Kuechly entered the 2012 NFL Draft. He could stop other teams from running the ball and defend the pass. That made him a rare linebacker who could stay on the field in any situation. The Carolina Panthers selected him with the ninth pick in the draft. Kuechly signed a four-year, $12.5 million **contract**. Just as he had in college, he was about to take the NFL by storm.

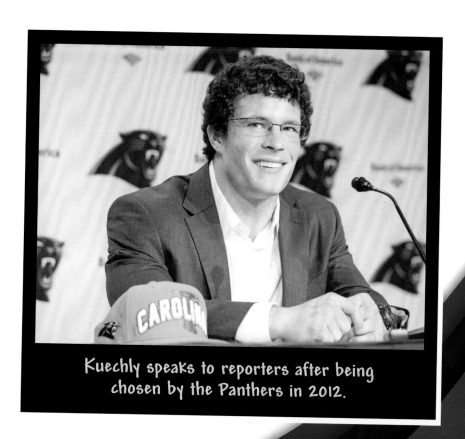

Kuechly speaks to reporters after being chosen by the Panthers in 2012.

Kuechly works hard to be ready for every game.

Kuechly's physical skills make him an ideal linebacker. He's strong enough to fight through opposing players, yet quick enough to knock down passes. But what really sets him apart is his mental approach to football and fitness.

Kuechly credits preparation for his success. It starts in the film room. Kuechly spends hours each week watching game film. He breaks down his own performance. He looks for areas where he can improve. And he studies his next opponent. He watches for patterns. He sees what other teams like to do, and he plans ways to stop them.

Spending many hours in the film room has helped make Kuechly one of the smartest players on the field.

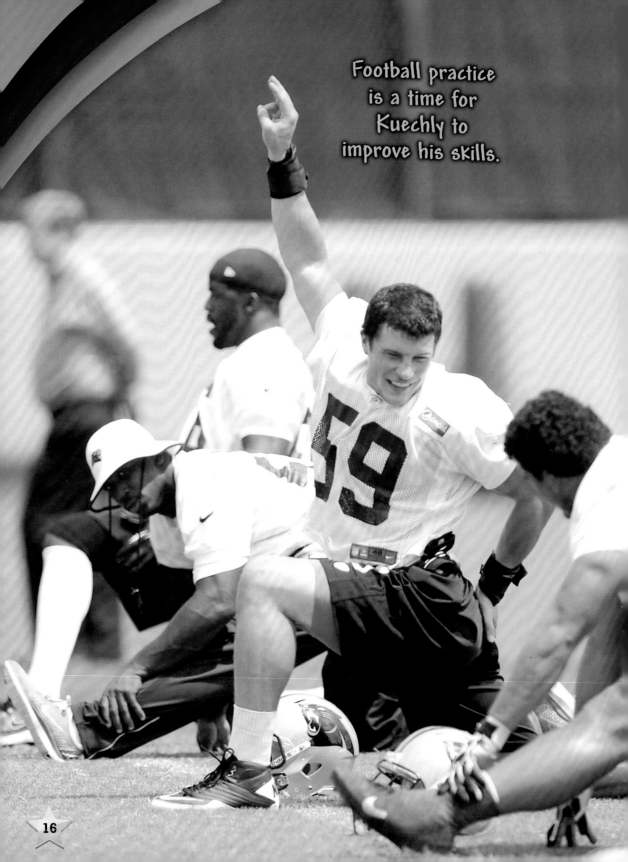

Football practice
is a time for
Kuechly to
improve his skills.

Kuechly watches so much film that Panthers head coach Ron Rivera once had to kick him out of the film room. It was Christmas Eve, and the linebacker was the only player left in the building. "I had to send him home," Rivera said. "He's so serious about who he is and what he wants to become and that's why he's special."

Kuechly keeps his body in peak physical condition. His training starts with stretching. Kuechly lifts weights to build muscle. **Cardio** training such as running and working on a rowing machine helps keep his lungs and heart in shape.

Kuechly stretches his muscles before a game. Stretching helps prevent injury.

Kuechly wears a sling to protect his injured left shoulder while watching a basketball game in 2016.

In 2015, Kuechly's workout plan took a detour. He had injured his shoulder during the 2014–2015 season. After surgery, he was unable to lift weights. Instead, he focused on getting ready mentally. He also exercised with stretchy bands. The bands provided a good workout without risking further injury to Kuechly's shoulder.

Diet is a big part of Kuechly's plan. Many people think of a diet as a way to lose weight. But for Kuechly, diet is a way to maintain his weight. As a linebacker, his body takes a lot of punishment. If he gets too light, he's more likely to be injured. Kuechly plans his diet around healthful foods that give him the energy he needs to build muscle. And he eats a lot. Kuechly may have five or six full meals in a day! He also drinks lots of water. While he usually stays away from junk food, Kuechly admits to one weakness—cookies and cream ice cream.

Diet and exercise help Kuechly build muscle.

When he's not playing, Kuechly is friendly and polite.

On the field, Kuechly is fierce. But according to teammates, that mean streak disappears as soon as he steps off the field. "Luke's the nicest guy I've ever met in my life," said former teammate Roman Harper.

Kuechly isn't married. But he has a longtime girlfriend, Gardner-Webb University student Shannon Reilly. Reilly is from Cincinnati, where Kuechly went to high school. Like Kuechly, she stays out of the spotlight as much as possible.

Kuechly's wholesome image has earned him some nicknames. Panthers quarterback Cam Newton calls him Captain America. Newton's nickname is Superman, and some teammates joke that Kuechly is like Clark Kent. The linebacker's strong chin and clean-cut style remind them of Superman's other half. But Kuechly seems to become a whole new person when he puts his football uniform on. The nice guy is replaced by a defensive superhero.

Many NFL players thrive on their fame. Kuechly isn't one of them. He tends to avoid the spotlight.

He keeps his private life private. He has always loved to be outdoors. Kuechly spends much of his free time fishing, camping, and hunting. He also hangs out with teammates. He has said that friendships off the field help players work together on it.

Back to School

Kuechly joined the NFL after his junior year of college. Even though he signed a contract for more than $12 million, he wasn't done with school. Kuechly continued taking classes. In 2015, he earned his degree in business marketing. "It's really important finishing what you start," he explained.

Kuechly took classes at Boston College to complete his degree. He also took classes on the Internet.

Kuechly (right) has fun with a young fan.

Kuechly steps into the public eye in his work with charities. In 2013, he became a spokesman for Project Life. The group helps people donate **bone marrow** and other body parts to people in need. In 2015, Kuechly surprised Panther fan Jessica Hayes by appearing at her 21st birthday party. Hayes suffers from several life-threatening medical conditions. Kuechly brought Hayes flowers and sang "Happy Birthday" at her party.

HERO

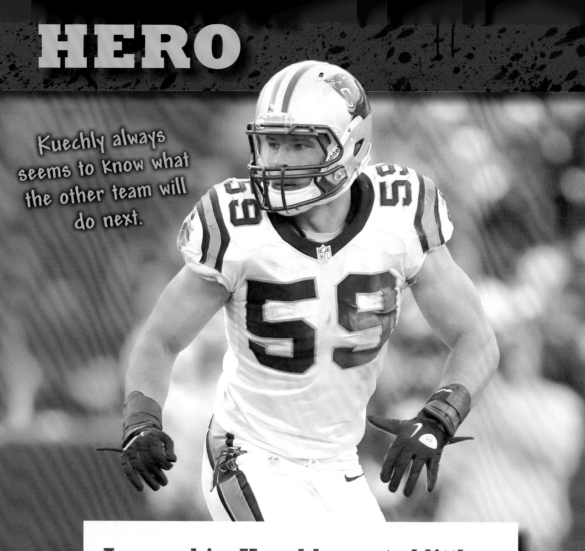

Kuechly always seems to know what the other team will do next.

As a rookie, Kuechly wasted little time making his mark in the NFL. His 164 tackles in 2012 led the league, and he was named the Defensive Rookie of the Year. In 2013, Kuechly was the heart of one of the league's top defenses. His ability to stop the run and cover passes made him a rare dual threat. He was named NFL Defensive Player of the Year.

Kuechly's greatest game may have come in week 16 of the 2013 season. The Panthers needed a victory to clinch a playoff spot. Kuechly dashed all around the field. He intercepted a pass. And he made tackle after tackle. The Carolina linebacker ended the game with 24 tackles, an NFL record. Better yet, the Panthers won the game, 17–13.

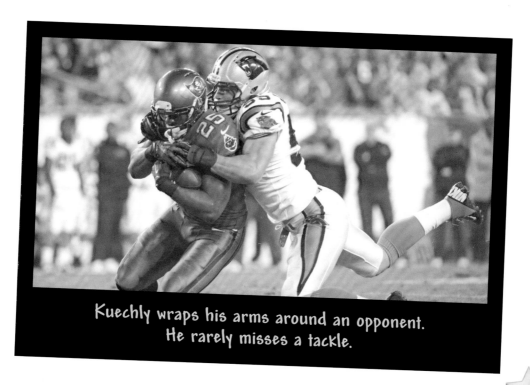

Kuechly wraps his arms around an opponent. He rarely misses a tackle.

Before the 2015 season, Kuechly signed a $62 million contract to stay with the Panthers for five more years. It made him the highest-paid middle linebacker in the NFL. That season, Kuechly missed the first games of his career. He suffered a **concussion** and sat out three games. But once he was back on the field, he and the Panthers cruised to victory after victory.

On Thanksgiving Day, Kuechly scored the first touchdown of his NFL career. Dallas Cowboys quarterback Tony Romo fired a pass down the field. Kuechly picked off the pass and dashed 32 yards to the end zone.

Kuechly protects the ball as he runs for his first NFL touchdown.

The Panthers earned a spot in the playoffs. Kuechly scored touchdowns against the Seahawks and the Cardinals to help the Panthers advance to Super Bowl 50. He played well in the Super Bowl, making 10 tackles and sacking Denver Broncos quarterback Peyton Manning. But it wasn't enough. Denver beat Carolina, 24–10, to win the title.

Kuechly has already earned his place as one of the NFL's top defenders. He led his team to the biggest football game in the world. Yet he was just 25 years old when the 2016 season kicked off. That's the age when many players just begin to enter their prime.

Kuechly's hard work has paid off. If he can stay healthy, there's no limit to what he might achieve. How many more times can he lead the league in tackles? Can he lead his team back to the Super Bowl? Can the league's top middle linebacker actually get better than he already is? Carolina fans can't wait to find out.

All-Star Stats

Kuechly is one of the NFL's best tacklers. Every season, he's among the league's leaders in takedowns, even though tackles aren't an official NFL statistic. Perhaps his most impressive statistic came in 2012, when he led the NFL in tackles—as a rookie!

2012 NFL Tackling Leaders

164 tackles   Luke Kuechly, Carolina Panthers (first season)
148 tackles   NaVorro Bowman, San Francisco 49ers (third season)
148 tackles   Chad Greenway, Minnesota Vikings (sixth season)
147 tackles   Jerod Mayo, New England Patriots (fifth season)
145 tackles   Jerrell Freeman, Indianapolis Colts (first season)

Most Tackles in College Football since 2005

191 tackles   Luke Kuechly, Boston College, 2011
183 tackles   Luke Kuechly, Boston College, 2010
179 tackles   Jimmy Cottrell, New Mexico State, 2005
166 tackles   Dan Molls, Toledo, 2012
165 tackles   Chris Chamberlain, Tulsa, 2007
165 tackles   Matt Castelo, San Jose State, 2006

Source Notes

10   Marcus Hartman, "Carolina's Luke Kuechly Has Risen from 2-Star Recruit to NFL Star," *Fox Sports*, January 30, 2016, http://www.foxsports.com/nfl/story/super-bowl-50-luke-kuechly-nfl-star-carolina-panthers-2-star-recruit-020116.

11–12   ESPN.com staff, "Young BC Linebacker Quietly among Nation's Best," *ESPN*, November 10, 2009, http://espn.go.com/blog/acc/post/_/id/6425/young-bc-linebacker-quietly-among-nations-best.

17   Ron Clements, "Christmas Eve Film Study Has Made Luke Kuechly a Complete Linebacker," *sportkix*, accessed July 22, 2016, https://www.sportkix.com/news/nfc-championship-cardinals-panthers-azvscar-luke-kuechly-cam-newton-ron-rivera.

20   Adam Kilgore, "If You're a Panther, Luke Kuechly Loves You. If Not, He'll Try to Crush You," *Washington Post*, January 25, 2016, https://www.washingtonpost.com/news/sports/wp/2016/01/25/if-youre-a-panther-luke-kuechly-loves-you-if-not-hell-try-to-crush-you/.

22   "Luke Kuechly Is Clark Kent in Cleats," Lott IMPACT Trophy, accessed July 22, 2016, http://lottimpacttrophy.org/luke-kuechly-is-clark-kent-in-cleats/.

Glossary

Atlantic Coast Conference (ACC): a group of college football teams that play against one another. The ACC includes Boston College and Florida State University.

bone marrow: a soft substance inside bones that makes white blood cells

cardio: a type of workout designed to get the heart pumping and improve blood flow

concussion: a brain injury caused by a hard hit on the head

contract: a written agreement between two or more parties, such as a player and a team

middle linebacker: a player on defense who lines up behind the line of scrimmage and usually plays in the middle of the field. Middle linebackers often direct other players on defense.

outside linebacker: a player on defense who lines up behind the line of scrimmage and usually plays on one side of the field

Pro Bowls: NFL all-star games

recruit: a high school player who is being considered by college teams

safety: a player on defense who usually lines up behind the linebackers

scouts: people who judge the abilities of football players

Further Information

Boston College Eagles Football
http://www.bceagles.com/index.aspx?path=football

Braun, Eric. *Super Football Infographics*. Minneapolis: Lerner Publications, 2015.

The Carolina Panthers
http://www.panthers.com

Challen, Paul C. *What Does a Linebacker Do?* New York: PowerKids, 2015.

Fishman, Jon M. *Cam Newton*. Minneapolis: Lerner Publications, 2017.

NFL Rush
http://www.nflrush.com

Wyner, Zach. *Carolina Panthers*. New York: AV2 by Weigl, 2015.

Index

Photo Acknowledgments

The images in this book are used with the permission of: © iStockphoto.com/63151 (gold and silver stars); Jim Dedmon/Icon Sportswire CDA/Newscom, p. 2; Jacob Kupferman/Cal Sport Media/Newscom, p. 4; Jeremy Brevard/USA Today Sports/ Newscom, p. 6; © Mike Ehrmann/Getty Images Sport/Getty Images, p. 7; © Jim Owens/Icon Sportswire, pp. 8, 9; © Ric Tapia/Icon Sportswire, p. 11; Mark Box/ ZUMApress/Newscom, p. 12; AP Photo/Chuck Burton, pp. 13, 23; © Charlotte Observer/Zumapress/Icon Sportswire, p. 14; © John Tlumacki/The Boston Globe/ Getty Images, p. 15; David T. Foster III/MCT/Newscom, p. 16; Chris Szagola/Cal Sport Media/Newscom, p. 17; © Streeter Lecka/Getty Images Sport/Getty Images, p. 18; © Joe Robbins/Getty Images Sport/Getty Images, p. 19; © Taylor Hill/Getty Images, p. 20; Jeff Siner/MCT/Newscom, p. 22; AP Photo/Damian Strohmeyer, p. 24; AP Photo/Phelan M. Ebenhack, p. 25; Brad Loper/TNS/Newscom, p. 26.

Front cover: Jim Dedmon/Icon Sportswire CDA/Newscom (Luke Kuechly); © iStockphoto.com/63151 (gold and silver stars); © iStockphoto.com/neyro2008 (motion lines); © iStockphoto.com/ulimi (black and white stars).